The Geography of Jazz

The Geography of Jazz

Lenard D. Moore

BLAIR

To all Jazz Artists,

Jazz Historians,

Jazz Critics,

Jazz Teachers,

and

Poets

for broadening our
appreciation of Jazz
and enriching
our human condition

Contents

Acknowledgments

Grateful appreciation is offered to the editors and publishers of the following publications in which some of these poems (in different versions) have previously appeared or are forthcoming:

Chautauqua: "Swinging Cool." Reprinted by permission of *Chautauqua*. Copyright 2014, Lenard D. Moore.

Black American Literature Forum (now, *African American Review*): "Raleigh Jazz Festival, 1986."

Raleigh: A Guide to North Carolina's Capital, 2nd Edition (The Raleigh Fine Arts Society, 1992): "Raleigh Jazz Festival, 1986."

Word and Witness: 100 Years of North Carolina Poetry (Carolina Academic Press, 1999): "Raleigh Jazz Festival, 1986."

Kola: A Black Literary Magazine (Canada): "Raleigh Jazz Festival, 1986."

NCArts Journal, Volume 15 Number 2 Winter 2001 (North Carolina Arts Council): "Raleigh Jazz Festival, 1986."

Fives: Fifty Poems by Serbian and American Poets, A Bilingual Anthology (Contact Line and Cross-Cultural Communications, 2002): "Raleigh Jazz Festival, 1986."

27 Views Of Raleigh: The Capital City in Prose & Poetry (Eno Publishers, 2013): "Raleigh Jazz Festival, 1986."

Furious Flower: African American Poetry from the Black Arts Movement to the Present(University of Virginia Press, 2004): "Girl Tap Dancing," originally titled "Black Girl Tap Dancing."

Swaying in Wicked Grace: A Collection Commemorating 25 Years of Furious Flower (James Madison University, 2019): "At the Train Stop."

Poetry: An Introduction, 5th Edition (Bedford/St. Martin's, 2007): "Girl Tap Dancing," originally titled "Black Girl Tap Dancing."

The Bedford Introduction To Literature, 8th Edition (Bedford/St. Martin's, 2008): "Girl Tap Dancing," originally titled "Black Girl Tap Dancing."

The Compact Bedford Introduction To Literature, 8th Edition (Bedford/St. Martin's, 2009): "Girl Tap Dancing," originally titled "Black Girl Tap Dancing."

The Griot: "Sunday Evening."

All That Jazz: "No Reply," originally titled "After Receiving No Reply."

A Long And Winding Road: "No Reply," originally titled "After Receiving No Reply."

Raleigh News & Observer: "Zora Shango."

Frogpond (The Journal of the Haiku Society of America): "Jazz Suite."

Near South: "Carolina Miles."

Pembroke Magazine: "Nneena Freelon In Raleigh."

Connotation Press: An Online Artifact: "At The Train Stop."

Home Is Where: An Anthology of African American Poetry From The Carolinas (Hub City Press, 2011): "At The Train Stop."

A Long And Winding Road: "At The Train Stop."

Obsidian: Literature In The African Diaspora: "Ascension: John Coltrane" and "Cookin.' "

Spillway 22: "Thursday Night."

Broadside published in an edition of one hundred fifty for the author's reading on March 21, 2000, at North Carolina Wesleyan College, with the title caption as *From Word and Witness* (Carolina Academic Press, 1999): "Raleigh Jazz Festival, 1986."

A Note of Thanks

For reading these poems in manuscript form, thanks to my former professor Gerald W. Barrax, Carolyn Beard Whitlow, Jan Zaleski Hilton (WSWG Member), Robin M. Caudell, DeLana R.A. Dameron (CAAWC Member), Adrienne Christian (CAAWC Member), Crystal Simone Smith (CAAWC Member), Ebony Noelle Golden (CAAWC Member), Tom Lombardo, Carolyne Wright and Gina M. Streaty (CAAWC Member). Also, thanks to Jerry W. Ward, Jr., Carole Boston Weatherford (CAAWC Member), Sally Ann Drucker (WSWG Member) Opal J. Moore, Bruce Lader (WSWG Member) and Jill Gerard for reading some of these poems and offering advice on them. In addition, thanks to the Carolina African American Writers' Collective, the Washington Street Writers Group and Cornelius Eady, Toi Derricotte, E. Ethelbert Miller, Marilyn Nelson, Eugene B. Redmond and Everett Hoagland for encouragement and friendship. Thanks to Ce Rosenow and Allise Penning at Mountains & Rivers Press for their support of this book.

The Geography of Jazz

Swinging Cool

The bassist hugs
the bass, plunks it.
Ting, boom, ting boom —
the drummer beats
and booms. Saxophonist
weaves notes, oscillates, blows
and the pianist finger-dances
on the keys: 'Swinging
at the Haven.' Musicians spark
the sheet music stands
and angled microphones.
Blue backdrop.
Modulating that tempo,
they work the tune.
Drumsticks knocking time,
piano plucking our ears.
Bassman still hugging
the bass, straight sets —
walls thrumming —
steady as the spring moon
inciting the indigo sky.

Raleigh Jazz Festival, 1986

On Fayetteville Street Mall
a lean man bobs his head.
His sax shines — polished
copper in a sunbeam,
rhythm, a splendid rising
echoing against concrete.

The trumpeter inches
across the homemade platform;
his angled jaw swerves
and slacks.
His notes — perfect
geometry for dancing.

People snap their fingers;
they are bassline
vibrating autumn.
Pigeons peck peanuts,
drum beaks
on the sidewalk.

The musicians blast into sky,
ripple red leaves loose
from a stand of trees,
glow in the sunset,
play vamps
as earthlings will do.

Tanka Note

Duke Ellington on piano
shadows everywhere
the black and white
the thin bookmark
against the door panel

DECEMBER 28, 1996

[5]

Cookin'
(at Mary Lou Williams Center)

Soprano sax sears
the upright stand
the bass boils
the piano simmers
the percussions baste
bubbling the chambers
of receptive hearts
chord changes flip
spin us from circular chairs
we release the steam
give way to dark notes
in autumn night
our eyes close, our hearts
full of harmonies
our spirits rise
to the diamond-shaped
tiles of the café ceiling
like balloons

escaping

Girl Tap Dancing
(for Cynthia M. Gary)

She taps, pats, clicks,
Shoes dazzling the checkered floor,
Arms whirl, whirl,
Legs cross, uncross,
Notes of the feet rise
Off tile,
Shoot toward the ceiling.

She pats, clicks, taps
Riffing the floor with her shoes,
Arms defy gravity,
Legs scissor perfectly,
Feet notes soar
Over the floor,
Scatter from table to table.

She clicks, pats, taps
Shoes shocking the floor,
Arms swirl, whirl,
Legs stamp, swing,
Feet notes smoke, beat
The floor, the floor.

She taps, clicks, pats,
This sister firing the floor,
Arms encompass endless circles,
Legs slide, glide,
Displace air, filling space,
Black feather bobbing as she taps.

Sunday Evening

(for Ramsey Lewis)

As lights glow red
in the distant background,
he sits at the great
black grand.
Fingers flutter across the keys.
Two black men
pluck their guitars'
tight, gold strings
and the percussionist
tings the cymbals —
their heads bob.
The audience claps.

Band members pat
their shiny black shoes.
The silver, gold
instruments gleam
brighter than the spotlight
beaming down
on the glossy stage.
The piano's chords
in tune, intone
better than, oh yes,
than any heart thump.

Genius's eyeglasses
follow his fingers'
every moment —
ah, the harmony.
Now Genius, tall
and lean, stands, bows
then thumps
onto the seat
and thumbs
the piano.
Man,
his pants, the
color of the piano,
sway
as if the wind beats them.
No one in the audience sits
without bobbing their heads
as the music progresses,
while the band's shadowed
heads rock
on curtains
turn purple,
then red.
Everyone walks off stage,
except the drummer,
who does his thing,

drumming
until the others come
back, back playing again.
That harmony
peels the walls bare.
Oh, I love, love it.
Can't you hear it too,
my friends?
They jammin'.
Every now and then,
the audience erupts.
The tilted man makes
that bass talk that talk.
My feet tap
against the tile floor.
Everybody's fingers pop, snap-pop,
popping on
into the chill night.

Listen,
let these words, words throb,
throb in your head
until you let go
of your rocking,
clapping self.

No Reply

sunk into the cord of night
maybe it was late
I talked by phone
into the hum of powerlines
into the Twice Told Coffeehouse
into the time
of your eardrum
my chords coiling
till the receiver had
only itself to listen

Zora Shango

Words float
from blues /
indigo-lit sheets
of paper

silk
spins vocal breath,
swaying symbols
of script:

she slow-drags notes
from the clarinet
of her throat
into winter air

her voice resonates
off cinder block
gym walls
fills our ear
drums

reverberates
this modulating night
this modulating night
reverberates

Bending back
she stomps
the stage-planks
again, again

Her caftan levitates
the mike bobs
around the stand
and she scats
and she scats

Ray Charles Accepts Honorary Degree

Shaw University, May 13, 2000

With help, he climbs the stage.
They stand. A community crowd.

Clapping. An ovation.
The black piano's

bars resonate.
The crowd bows.

King Charles
rocks back and forth,

a royal song.
Over Ray's raspy syllables,

graduates scream in tribute,
dance.

Four-year prayers,
lights

in this civic center.
Graduates sway, shine, revere —

an audience of old faces
blending in tone, in air.

How Rhythm Bends River Like

Pain stamps 'Giant Steps'
up my back faster than
the haunting horn.

Midnight. The music spins
on time. The musician strokes,

fingers the thick-black Carolina night.
Listen how rhythm bends river-like,
surges

before day spills again,
before the rooster's quake
floats and breaks, floats and breaks
on the air, the air, air,
air, oh yes, floating and breaking air.

Greenbriar Mall, East Point

My people, I watch come and go.
Your brown art I admire —

long sepia braids celebrating
the hot body of Atlanta.

Seated in the food court
across from Medu Bookstore,

I catch harmony from my people
who rhythm this Saturday evening,

radiating summer-gold sun
in reds, black, greens

I am these people, coming, going,
and they are me, us, them, we.

Reading the Black Poets

I, too, am reading *The Black Poets*
in the rhythm of the floor fan.
I like to conjure the place
where the reading takes me —
grateful for the booming day
when Dudley Randall let Black voices sing
the flurry of times,
the flurry of times.
I say I, too, am reading *The Black Poets* —
an ensemble of beating drums
in the sacred temple of my body.

Alchemy of New Orleans & San Francisco

I hear a poem, Bob Kaufman
   speaks from the page,
mind full of spontaneity
   & vowels scattering
while he shimmies
   till the moon rises,
a big bright eye
   in the black brush sky.

   Maybe it was New Orleans
pulsing & drawing him
   into double dares:
night rhythms.

A net of sound
   pulls me
into Parker walking Kaufman home
   & controlling time
as if cadence were a fish, caught
   in the globed face
of May's misty moon.

   Maybe it was San Francisco
waxing & wearing
   his flesh
across the years,
   necessary as gills respiring.

After Hours Jook Joint

for Yusef Komunyakaa

Deejay spins Ramsey Lewis
on the turntable, whips
chords out of black & white keys
melodies of history
that pool in our ears.
His fingers break sound
from the grooves in the vinyl
till this room fills with smoke.
Our pain floats away
on the dance floor.
Ramsey — he just grooves,
hexing scores like
a woman's strut, full of swing
in the twirling spotlight.

Barwell Road

These dark notes
falling and breaking
in my ears
would claim me
if they had heart and brain.
The cool El Nino
band's improvising
pulls me into time,
stars throb
a beat that knocks
in my feet, tries
to mark me like days
when city clouds hung heavy
over the highway.
This music reels me;
the compact car,
a closed box
blowing pain like wind.

Thursday Night

Needle on vinyl,
Miles in the groove,
& ghosts hover
over the warped wooden shelf.
I feel *Summertime,*
now full of mood & pain,
sustaining turns in my heart
till that trumpet speaks
like a howl yowled on wind
as the Carolina moon
beams into this cold room.
This music heats me
like bad booze burns,
like promises never kept:
I listen all night long
as ancestors keep watch,
bob in and out on unsettling vibes.

Mesmerized

She struts riveting beats
down sidewalk slopes

through campus courtyard
while rain mists her hair —

sable locks swing
across her black blouse.

Red pumps stamp
a slender-legged salsa

while wet willows wave
like hands, stirred men

eyeing the woman's blue jeans —
tight as a goatskin drum.

Jazz Suite

Spring cleaning —
tracery of dust on the Duke
Ellington bookmark

An Armstrong refrain
A meadowlark circles
the campus courtyard

steamy evening...
shadows plastering
all the café walls

August heat —
a record warps
on the dashboard

quartet
in the courtyard —
hazy stars

alone with the moon
concentric circle of dust
on old records

ladybug
on the lamp shade —
last bars of piano

late winter —
a vibraphone opens the set
inside the arena

Dizzy Gillespie Plays at the Jazz Hall

His jaws a double bubble
wider than the trumpet's mouth
opening.
They might pop
beneath the lights.
His forehead gleams
like the brass he holds.
Gillespie bends into the microphone.

My heart, his horn,
pulse improvisations,
quicken with the rhythms
spreading on the air,
my head tilted,
the horn in Gillespie's hands
fills my heart, it might pop
with a sound too great.
It drives me dizzy.

A Note on Improvisations

Some chord-sweet notes enter my eardrum and reel me
into longing for its woman-mellow voice while I sit under a
Carolina moon in Moore Square as the gold acorn
sculpture loses its form in swallowing darkness in this
capital city of oaks where fallen shadows lead me slowly
back into my childhood when dark shapes played on our
bedroom walls at night improvising in our house of nature
till day breaks in the room

Wednesday Night at the Renaissance Hotel

In the center Oliver Lake
moves the horn up
and down into quick talk.
The man on steel drums
strikes till his long locks dance.
And another man in all-black
fingers the red guitar
into green string chords.
The other man on percussion
rocks, his beat booming
time into the midnight ballroom.
Oliver Lake turns the mike
into a fourth dimension.
I am inside the music:
my ascent — like a jet
above earth — edging
the billowed-bed of clouds.
And I love taking this ride,
almost reaching the stars,
not wanting to turn back,
my arms, wings,
stretched out, gliding
to the harmony, hands open.
Oliver incites, then floats
the horn away from his lips —
drinking the drums and guitar.

Then Lake spits melody,
his horn saying 'Oh yeah, Oh yeah'
to the tall black speakers
like trees at midnight
flanking the stage.

The Idea of Elegance

Eyes closed in pouring light,
Nancy Wilson's voice mellows
the piano accompaniment,
takes us
into a combo of night sweats
bright as diamonds draping
her sleeveless black dress.
She sings 'Autumn Leaves'
and conjures love to cipher like
language that measures her lips.
She lifts her left hand
into a dissipating sound.
We are black and white keys.

Hudson Valley Writers' Center

a man pushes
a blue baby carriage

the sound of the river
laps the shore

afternoon crickets chit
chat the wind

docked boats bob
a chipmunk descends

the concrete steps
to the train stop

where Metro North
comes and goes

a bird ascends autumn
three musicians unpack the black

van backed
to the shellacked door

where we will converge
on an evening

of poetry and music,
moods and movements

American Jazzku

(96th Street Library, New York City)

We sit in a hush so deafening
it tingles my ears
for what will burst
into talk,
into poems.

Quartet at Smoke
(2751 Broadway, New York City)

Trombone covers
black head of the mike
its slide, the slim gold arm
almost strikes my head
at our candlelit table
Tenor Saxophone takes
in the long gray nose
of the other mike
Congas smack
in the back corner
of the velvet-red stage
B3 Organ pumps
the bird-quick chords
in spotlight

I am in awe
how the bone man
bends back branch-like,
still dazzles,
the way the percussionist
strikes again and again
the way the tenor saxophonist
holds a note
the way the organ accentuates
black and white keys
rising grace

Cigarette smoke curls
around tonal color,
first set sends me
into a frenzy
in this dim club
where Picasso watches
from the lithograph
on the brick wall
like grace notes
cling to the drums
of my ears
in uptown Manhattan

Lenox Lounge
(Harlem, NY)

Horn arrangement:
Roy Campbell, flugelhorn,
Kenny Williams, alto sax,
trumpet Melvin Vines,
leads:
Andrew Bemkey piano
sustains soft sounds
Chris Sullivan on bass
rocks, shakes
as if possessed
Mike Thompson, drums,
sticks flying
left eye closes
rhythm
lifts
the lounge
an aura
of tonal light
and texture

Others join the jam:
Wes Reynoso on piano
Sam Gresham sits in
on drums
Kenyatta Beasley on trumpet

They harmonize
then fade
come back again
as we hover
like spirits
above tables
portrait of Fitzgerald
over my right shoulder
staring

Saco alto
Yasuma sax
leans
her interlude,
converges
on stage
bamboo Shu-Ni
Tsou flute
fingers quick
as hummingbird wings
other musicians
catch her rhythm
then let her solo
join her
swinging tempo
right on time
right
on time

At Duke Chapel

(Sunday, September 21, 2003)

Carmen Lundy sings
'Glory To God'
in the company
of pews filled
with witnesses.
Behind her,
the ensemble,
in formal black and white,
takes the chorus line.
The drummer strikes time,
tempo grabbing our hearts.
Walls bear her voice —
keepers of old truths.
Straight-backed,
she turns us out and out;
her aura of notes
climbs.
She closes her eyes
to tangerine sweet
geometry of ceiling light.
How we ascend,
like applause,
like thunder,
or fall like rain
through time of chill
this temple incites.

Inherit the Light

(Sunday, September 21, 2003)

Carmen Lundy, in black dress,
sings to angels,
does not need the mike,
but it demands her;
Buster Williams' bass
lays down the rhythm,
as she calls 'Lazarus'
with Geri Allen's melody
and moves toward hush
in bent ears of autumn Sunday
as we sit inheriting light.

Geri,
elegant in her red dress,
eases grace
from the piano
as if tune were sermon.
In coolness, beneath ceiling light,
the music-message resonates
as we listen to chords
billowing.
When Carmen's crescendo
surrounds us,
seated in the pews,
the stained windows waver.

Carolina Miles

An ice storm
tattoos the time.
I lie next to my woman
beneath blanket layers.
Piano bars slowly
seduce our hearts.
'Blue in Green' serenades
the bedroom. We do not
know icicles
mated to vinyl eaves.
The trumpet reels us
into a craze
of lovemaking;
summer sizzles
in our bedroom.
Winter taps against
windows. We ignore
pings, take ourselves
into rhythm,
our breathing:
slow and easy.
We are in blue
mood of one
plus one: together.

We are in green
hour: body heat.
This is trumpet
Talk: 'Blue in Green,'
'Blue in Green.'

Eros and Jazz

'Blue In Green'
spills liquid
from speakers.
I remember
I am home alone.
I'd rather
hold my woman
than this pen,
buckle ourselves
into long cantillating
love serenades.
The tune arouses
slow dance memory:
breath to breath
hearts in sync
like Miles' ensemble.
Now it's drizzling,
the all-day kind.
Cold, too.
The music and I
wait out her return,
all grace and timbre
as my shadow clings
to the windowpane, pulses.
A heart, lips,
Arms. Again
and again early spring
leaks.

Cassandra Swings Back

You hug your guitar
Contralto moan about
getting on the train
your white smile
pulls me
from my chair
your black pants
the strength of your
blonde dreadlocks swings
throaty voice swings back
I too lean back
and feel you turning
closed-eyed
and fingering my hair
your strings my beard
late night when wind
weeps from floor
fans like crazed notes
like me floating/
drifting

Nneena Freelon in Raleigh

Your voice comes
straight at us
Even the silence
of your pause
is tuned
Your timing
flirts with the bass
while you sing
'I Thought about You'
You lean
into a scat
permit the key
to fiddle our hearts
You send worries
away
grace us
with another song
You open your palms
reshape the air
with long fingers
Fluid hands sing —
Your lyrics tingle
inside me
become blood pulsing

I don't want you to leave
the auditorium
your indigo voice flips
notes on my tongue
but I can't give them back
don't want to
This sultry night
they become the stars

The Literary Salon

In the sconce-lit lounge
we curl in cushioned chairs,
cock our ears
to the record player,
the cadence of Langston Hughes
spilling from 12 *Moods for Jazz*.
We read from *The Collected Poems
of Langston Hughes*,
the winding river of his life.
The baby grand piano waits
like the jazz-black poster
on the beige bulletin board.
We read, flip pages, read,
and at the same sweet time
the LP spins,
the shadow of a moth
circles the ceiling.

Intermission, 1956
(after a photograph / for Billie Holiday)

Lady, you seem starved,
pastel dress drooped
from your bony shoulders.

Your face speaks:
three furrows line your brow,
your mouth —a parted blossom.

Your left hand holds a tissue,
your right clutches sheet music.
From your mouth a cigarette drops ashes.

Smoke laces
the song you will sing
in Carnegie Hall,

fingers the bracelet glistening
on your wrist, perfumes
your diamond earrings.

Stars would dim
if they knew
how you gaze backstage.

What walks you
into a still night
at the end of sky?

Spillways

Traveling south,
a Branford Marsalis tune tears
from the car radio,
his horn bending
a stream of notes,
drizzle tapping the windshield
as lightly as my woman's fingers
touch my face,
her lips press
against my cheek
until we arrive
finally at the hotel
where faces lift
amid notes about poetry,
though music
binds us
to the softness of our chairs
and the curtain closes out
twilight spilling beyond the window.

Lovebeat

My eyes close like blinds
I pull shut in her bedroom
as she draws me close enough
to stroke my lips.
'Take me,' she nods
as if pulling notes
from Miles's horn.
Coltrane's music is gentle,
rain quenching jazzbuds open.

Echoes of Sarah's Words

Craning the same way
as the lectern-mike
you see hundreds of eyes
scanning your face,
the contour of your bright presence.
This is when I soar,
a bluebird in a trance.
I don't hear the words
responding to my call —
or hear the silence
between them. If
I catch cadence right
in all that stunning
light, I sway,
swing —
blue as a mood indigo sky.

Songbird

Dianne Reeves knocks me out:
'You're Driving Me Crazy'
streams summer-like
with late-night chords.
I see a green flame.
I can't stop the lyrics
from turning me in & out.
She tugs my strings
to snapping point.
All I can see is jade.
I become a stand of willows,
bow into notes,
with emerald grace.
The piano cannot touch her
harmony, painting me slowly.

The Blue Room

(18th & Vine, Kansas City, Missouri)

The wall — a gallery of
Black and white photographs.
Genius peered at us,
starry eyes piercing darkness.

Lester Young, beaming
with light, stilled us.
No one wanted to turn away;
his pitch alterations stunned.

This tenor, who gigged
at the Cherry Blossom,
played in Count Basie's band,
his swinging sax always leaping.

The night dissipated in the city.
Indigo, the splashing ink,
washed the sky all morning
as if Young gave nuance.

Now, the wall's rich reach of photos stretching
from our knees to almost ceiling
reveals every artist who sang, scatted
and synchronized tunes in this club.

If you will, imagine us flipping like cards.
We're three generations of kin
witnessing and reeling — one of us remembering
those live times when mouths piped notes like steam.

At the Train Stop

I imagine the quick hand:
Thelonious Monk waves
at red, orange, yellow leaves
from Raleigh to Rocky Mount.
Alone in this seat,
I peer out the half-window
at the rainbow of faces
bent toward this train
that runs to the irresistible Apple,
determine to imagine Monk
glows like Carolina sun
in cloudless blue sky.
I try so hard to picture him
until his specter hunkers
at the ghost piano, foxfire
on concrete platform.
Now I can hear the tune 'Misterioso'
float on sunlit air.
If notes were visible,
perhaps they would drift crimson,
shimmer like autumn leaves.
A hunch shudders
into evening, a wordless flight.

Max Roach Speaks to an Audiophile

I bebopped bass drums,
didn't want to keep my sticks

to beat regular,
wanted to extend

my scope, deepen my
accents, invent and

expand harmony.

I wanted fans' ears
filled with something new,

a different sky
each day. You got

to play for something, young
fellow. You know, work

outside of yourself.

I rode my cymbals
as if the last gig.

Nina Simone Speaks to a Connoisseur

I sang my own cuts.
I've worked with Don Pullen.
Ben Riley drummed for me,
I never wanted to be labeled.
I confused your ear with difference.
I wanted my vocals
to be signature. I wanted
to do Tryon
proud. So right.
'Don't Let Me Be Misunderstood'
took me to a spiritual plane.
Oh, I loved that piano.
I know some folk called me feisty,
but I wanted to extend my range,
explore something as vast as a blue sky.

Ascension: John Coltrane

I didn't pick up the tenor
and soprano saxophones
for legendhood.
I wanted only to explore chords
into progression, step into another world.
I had to escape anything too strict,
take 'Giant Steps' all the way
from Hamlet, North Carolina.
The music shimmered like a lake
inside me and turned blue.
It was kind of spiritual.
I thought of extending the scales.
I wanted to play on and on,
sail as long as the horn could
and eventually come back again
as if I had never left.
It was maybe the only time
I left my body.

Interlude

nothing but chops
baby, yes, chops
nothing but chops
yes, yes, yes
chops, nothing but
chops, baby, yes

New Orleans Suite

1. Evening

Tuesday,
not fat at all.
I arrive at
Louis Armstrong International,
expecting to hear
an Armstrong song
streaming
through hidden speakers:
or spot his portrait.
I mark distance
to baggage claims.
Unexpected whiffs
of heat, the day's best trick.
I quit my trench coat.
I improvise a November sky.

2. *Afternoon, The Next Day*

South Scott to Canal,
where mahogany men tar
sunlit stretch
of miles
for streetcars
I do not see.
I flirt with the flaring
thought of a silver
horn treading hundreds
of notes
as fierce almost as
my pounding feet.
I pull open
the door to Mandina's
restaurant. Eat a po'boy sandwich:
half fried shrimp, half fried oysters.
Night comes. My tongue still cradles
the buttered, lemony taste.
I walk the city's heart,
turning through heat,
swooning.
Above floats the creamy moon.

3. At Maple Leaf Bar

We talk to drums
thrumming their talk

Kermit Ruffins singing
in the nearby room

we listen
to the beat-voice
taking us
into twenty-first century
time timing time

Kermit's trumpet
telling Cajun secrets
in blissful night
when we wish
drums and horn
to levitate us, spent phones
receiving message
in smoky midnight
when ghosts tiptoe
among those who lend ears
to throated percussions

4. *Morning*

When I lie awake
in an iron frame bed,
the mattress shakes.
Ignore it.
I don't know what wants me
to rise like the southern sun.
Minutes creep. But shaking
becomes urgent, despite the shine
of light
over the foot of the bed.
Finally, my feet strike
shiny hardwood floor.
I shuffle to the mahogany desk,
try to write
with the pen, but
the glazed desk trembles
like a bad leg.
I sit in the antique chair,
give blood to words;
the page reddens.

5. Night

We traverse chilly night,
turn corners, cross crowded streets,
stamp the sidewalk,
four friends pushing deeper
into starry night.
The wind walks with us,
wraps us in its arms,
slaps my hatless head,
hunches on its shadow.
Not even jackets or trench coats
can stop the shivering.
Beneath the autumn moon,
we become tight knots walking.
Saints guide us.
We seek Café Du Monde,
but the distance does not shorten
fast enough.

6. At Café Du Monde

We sit at a table.
To our left, a man
with hair so bushy
his head can't be cold;
his beard hangs thick,
hue of half-past midnight.
'He's an artist,' says Ronald,
lifting his chocolate cup.
I study my beignet,
take a bite.
Vida looks at me,
smiles, says, 'See
how proper he eats.'
I laugh.
Powdered sugar spills
on my tan trench coat.
Our laughter trumpets.
I turn to see who else mimics.
'We make tourists laugh,' says Vida,
'so sugar will get all over them.'
Patrice nods.
Her glassy eyes swing.

I lean down
toward hot chocolate,
needing to know how I fell
for one trick in the night.
Now we rise.
Four of us walk
into the great city darkness
where wind strums us,
while the sidewalk drums
beneath our feet,
not because it wants to,
but because it has to.

7. On Bourbon Street

Windy throb of night.
We stand in long coats,
facing the open door.
Glistening gold in obsidian hands,
rhythmic horns persist,
an eruption.
The sweet, metallic sound
we seek: trumpets
flaring harmony.
We linger. Stars
punctuate the indigo sky.
This is how jazz allures:
a brilliant movement,
voluptuous music,
spreading, molten,
fluent
as a trail of smoke.
Blue birds blaze
midnight air.
We take flight.

About the Author

LENARD D. MOORE, founder and executive director of the Carolina African American Writers' Collective, is the author of *A Temple Looming* (WordTech Editions, 2008); *Desert Storm: A Brief History* (Los Hombres Press, 1993); *Forever Home* (St. Andrews College Press, 1992); and *The Open Eye* (Mountains & Rivers Press, 2015) and (North Carolina Haiku Society Press, 1985). He also is co-founder of the Washington Street Writers Group. He is former President of the Haiku Society of America (2008 and 2009). He is Executive Chairman of the North Carolina Haiku Society. His poems have appeared in *Callaloo, African American Review, Agni, Artful Dodge, Prairie Schooner, North American Review, Blues Revue Quarterly, Blues Access,* and elsewhere. His poems have also appeared in more than one hundred anthologies. He has performed his poetry with the jazz combo R.S.V.P. featuring Paul and Drew Laughlin on piano and bass, and Dick Day on drums, on Wednesday, April 23, 2003, at 8 p.m., at Otterbein College, in Westerville, Ohio. The program was titled 'Rhythm: An Evening of Jazz Poetry with Lenard D. Moore.' He has also performed his poetry accompanied by jazz pianist Vijay Iyer, saxophonist, clarinetist, and flutist J.D. Parran, and bassist Mark Deutsch, on Sunday, September 29th, 2002, at 3:15 p.m.- 6:15 p.m., in the Po'Jazz Series, at The Hudson Valley Writers' Center, in New York. In addition, he has read/performed his poetry accompanied by bassist Chris Sullivan, on Tuesday, October 1, 2002, at Manhattan College, in Riverdale, New York. Moreover, he has performed his poetry accompanied by The Joel Dias-Porter Quintet with Al Young on saxophone, Jay Jefferson on drums, Janelle Gill on piano, and Herm Burme on bass, on Friday, September 24, 2004, at The 2004 Furious Flower Poetry Conference, at James Madison University. Furthermore, he has read/performed his poetry accompanied by the Mount Olive College Symphonic Band and Jazz Band, on Thursday, November 1, 2012, at 7:30 p.m., at

Mount Olive College Assembly Hall, in Mount Olive, North Carolina. He has performed his poetry accompanied by The Matt Kendrick Trio with Michael Kinchen on tenor sax, John Wilson on drums, and Matt Kendrick on upright bass, on Saturday, December 15, 2012, at 8:00 p.m., at the Community Arts Café, in Winston-Salem, North Carolina. Then, too, he has read/performed his poetry with the accompaniment of jazz saxophonist James Dallas, on Tuesday, April 9, 2013, at 9:30 a.m., at Capitol West Academy, a charter school in Milwaukee. Later that evening (April 9, 2013), at 7:00 p.m., he performed his poetry accompanied by The Dennis Klopfer Jazz Trio with Bill Feldman on drums, Dennis Klopfer on piano, and Duane Stuermer on guitar, in Helfaer Hall at Mount Mary College, in Milwaukee, Wisconsin. He has also read/performed with other jazz bands. He is recipient of several awards, including The Haiku Society of America Merit Book Award for best anthology for editing *One Window's Light: A Collection of Haiku*, (Unicorn Press, 2017); North Carolina Award for Literature (2014); Eastern North Carolina Gilbert-Chappell Distinguished Poet (2009 and 2008); Raleigh Medal of the Arts for Lifetime Achievement in the Arts (2008); Sam Ragan Award in the Fine Arts (2006); Haiku Museum of Tokyo Award (2003, 1994 and 1983); Tar Heel Of The Week Award (Sunday, February 8, 1998); Margaret Walker Creative Writing Award (1997); and Indies Arts Award (1996). Moore is Associate Professor of English at University of Mount Olive where he teaches Advanced Poetry Writing and African American Literature.

This book has been designed & typeset
by Jonathan Greene in a new version
of W.A. Dwiggins' typeface Electra,
now named LfA Aluminia, created
by Jim Parkinson.

CPSIA information can be obtained
at www.ICGtesting.com
Printed in the USA
JSHW010857260720
6905JS00003B/12